THE #2020 VEGAN COOKBOOK

Delicious and Healthy Plant-Based Recipes for Every Day incl. Snacks on the Go

[1st Edition]

Andrew W. Ross

ISBN - 9798610122106

INTRODUCTION

INTRODUCTION

So you've decided to become a vegan, but where do you start? Working your way into a vegan way of life can seem very overwhelming; however, with just a little patience, you will see that it is not as challenging as you think. It's imperative to go at your own pace and to settle on a technique that works best for you. Here are a few thoughts and rules to structure your change to veganism, simply tailor them to your particular needs.

HOW TO START A VEGAN DIET

This is the place you have to genuinely consider what is best for you. Here are some great ways to get started:

- Cut out all meat from your eating routine, including fish and poultry. Take care not to substitute all meat with dairy and eggs as you will be cutting them out eventually as well.

- Keep away from items containing gelatin, rennet, and other products made of animal byproducts (barring dairy and eggs).

- Add in more whole grains, beans, vegetables, tofu, nuts, and seeds into your eating routine.

- Once you feel good about that, begin eliminating dairy and eggs.

HOW VEGAN EATING AFFECTS YOUR HEALTH

A well-adjusted, vegan diet unavoidably depends all the more vigorously on food sources that can add to a higher day by day contribution of valuable supplements. That is why there are a lot of great advantages you will see health-wise.

- Healthier heart

- Better BMI

- Less chance of diabetes

- Decreased inflammation

- Improved mental health and cognitive abilities

HOW THE DIET CHANGES YOUR BODY

The principal thing that somebody beginning a vegan diet may see is a boost of energy. The foods included in the diet will support your nutrient, mineral, and fiber levels. As time goes by, there is probably going to be an improvement in the internal workings. This is because of the higher fiber intake of a vegan diet, and the synchronous increment in starches in the gut and can have an impact on the inner workings. This may also prompt some positive changes in the variety of microscopic organisms in the colon.

INTRODUCTION

RECIPES

BREAKFAST

PORRIDGE BOWL

Servings: 1

INGREDIENTS

- 1 banana, pureed
- 1/4 tsp. of cinnamon
- 1/4 tsp. of maca powder
- A splash of vanilla extract
- 1/3 cup of coconut flour (78mL)
- 1/2 cup of hot oat milk (118mL)
- 1/2 cup of hot water (118mL)

DIRECTIONS

1. Combine bananas, cinnamon, vanilla, and maca in a blender. Mix until smooth
2. In a serving bowl, add the coconut flour and hot oat milk. Pour hot water over. Then add your blender mixture and stir.
3. Serve garnished with fresh fruit, more cinnamon, or even cocoa nibs.

Nutritional Facts:

Calories: 115
Proteins: 5.1g
Carbs: 17.4g
Fats: 3.1g

AUTUMNAL FRENCH TOAST

Servings: 4

INGREDIENTS

- 8 slices of whole-grain bread
- 3/4 cup of pumpkin puree (162g)
- 1.5 cups of unsweetened soy milk (355mL)
- 1 tbsp. of maple syrup
- 1 tbsp. of flax meal
- 1 tsp. cinnamon
- 1/4 tsp. of nutmeg
- 1/4 tsp. turmeric
- ground cloves, pinch

DIRECTIONS

1. Whisk all the ingredients together in a small bowl, except for the bread. Place a skillet on medium heat.
2. Dredge each slice of bread quickly in the mixture. Do not soak too long as it will make the bread soggy.
3. Cook until browned nicely and then flip the toast and repeat the process.

Nutritional Facts:
Calories: 405
Proteins: 19.2g
Carbs: 48.1g
Fats: 16.3g

VEGAN BREAKFAST HASH

Servings: 2

INGREDIENTS

- 4 potatoes, Yukon
- 1/2 of a bell pepper, red, diced
- 1/2 of a bell pepper, green, diced
- 1/2 of a bell pepper, yellow, diced
- 1/2 of a bell pepper, orange, diced
- 1/2 of an onion, red, thinly sliced
- 1/2 cup of mushrooms, chopped (75g)
- 1 cup of fresh spinach (178g)
- 1 tsp. of pepper
- 1/4 tsp. of salt
- 1/2 tsp. of Italian flavoring
- 1 tsp. of garlic powder
- 2 tbsp. of maple syrup

DIRECTIONS

1. Prepare all the vegetables. In a large skillet, melt the coconut oil over a medium-high heat. Layer potatoes in one evenly across the skillet bottom.
2. Allow to cook untouched for 2 minutes. Flip the potatoes and cook for an additional 2 minutes. Then mix them up and cook for 2 more minutes.
3. Lower the heat and throw in the peppers and onions. Mix together.
4. Include every one of your seasonings and mix well.
5. Add in the spinach and mushrooms. Cook for 2 minutes. Drizzle the maple syrup and cook until the spinach wilts. Take off the heat and serve with your favorite condiment or toppings.

Nutritional Facts:
Calories: 200
Proteins: 5g
Carbs: 27g
Fats: 9g

TOFU SCRAMBLE W/ GREEN PEPPERS

Servings: 4

INGREDIENTS

- 1 diced onion
- 1 diced bell pepper, green
- 1/2 of a jalapeño pepper, minced
- 1/4 cup of vegetable stock, low-sodium
- 1/4 tsp. of ground turmeric
- 2 tbsp. of nutritional yeast, flakes
- 1 tbsp. of garlic powder
- 1/4 tsp. of salt
- 1/4 tsp. of pepper
- 2 tbsp. of soy sauce, low-sodium
- 1 pkg. of extra firm tofu, drained and crumbled
- 3 tbsp. of parsley, fresh, chopped

DIRECTIONS

1. In a skillet on a medium-high heat, sauté the onion, pepper, and jalapeño in the vegetable stock. Cook until the vegetables become delicate, about 5 mins.
2. Add the seasonings and soy sauce. Keep cooking for 1–2 minutes longer.
3. Add the tofu and lower the heat. Cook for an extra 1–2 minutes.
4. Take off the stove and mix the parsley in. Serve right away.

Nutritional Facts:

Calories: 112
Proteins: 10.6g
Carbs: 11g
Fats: 3.9g

SAVORY BREAKFAST BOWL

Servings: 2

INGREDIENTS

Tofu Scramble
- 1 pkg of medium/firm tofu, crumbled
- 1tsp. of turmeric
- salt and pepper to taste
- soy sauce
- 1 tbsp. of water

Sautéed Veggies
- 1 bunch of kale, diced
- 1 cup mushrooms. Sliced (178g)
- 1/2 cup onion, diced (85g)
- 2 cloves of garlic, minced

The Bowls
- 1/2 avocado
- salsa
- 1/2 cup of brown rice (89g)

DIRECTIONS

1. Put all the tofu ingredients in one bowl and set aside.
2. Then add the veggies into a skillet over medium to high heat with either a sprinkle of water or a 1/2 tsp of your chosen cooking oil. Cook for 5-8 minutes, until the onions are translucent. Then remove them from the skillet and place in a bowl.
3. Add the tofu into the same skillet and cook for 5 minutes
4. Then assemble the bowls. Add a scoop of brown rice and then place it in the tofu and veggie mixtures. Top with avocado and a little dollop of salsa.

Nutritional Facts:
Calories: 373
Proteins: 16.3g
Carbs: 53.8g
Fats: 11.8g

PANCAKES

Servings: 2

INGREDIENTS

- 3 bananas, ripe
- 1 cup non-dairy milk, hemp (237mL)
- 2 cups oats, rolled (144g)

DIRECTIONS

1. Heat a skillet on a medium to low heat. Put all the ingredients into a blender and mix until batter consistency.
2. Pour a third of a cup of mixture into the skillet. Allow the pancake to cook until bubbles form around the edges, then turn over and cook for 2 mins until golden on each side. Then serve topped with your favorite fruit or syrup.

Nutritional Facts:
Calories: 306
Proteins: 21.1g
Carbs: 68.1g
Fats: 10.6g

VEGAN HUEVOS RANCHEROS TACOS

Servings: 2

INGREDIENTS

- 1 tsp. coconut oil
- 6 tortillas, corn
- 1 sm. pkg. firm tofu, crumbled
- 1 can of black beans, drained and rinsed
- 1/2 of cup salsa (116mL)
- 1 avocado, squashed
- Salt and pepper to taste
- 1 lime
- 1/2 cup of cilantro, fresh, chopped (53g)

DIRECTIONS

1. Heat some oil in a skillet and scramble the tofu, until lightly browned. Add salt and pepper to your taste. Remove and set to the side.
2. Heat more coconut oil (not too much) in a skillet on a medium to high heat. Add the beans and salsa. Mix until combined thoroughly. Season with salt and pepper.
3. Lower the heat and add in the tofu. While this is warming through, you can warm the tortillas in a small frying pan.
4. Then add in the tofu and bean mixture into the corn tortillas and top each with more salsa, crushed avocado, a squeeze of lime, and cilantro.

Nutritional Facts:
Calories: 384
Proteins: 14.1g
Carbs: 64.2g
Fats: 10.5g

CHARD & TOFU MUFFINS

Servings: 12

INGREDIENTS

Vegetable Mix
- Vegetable broth, low sodium
- 2 garlic cloves, chopped
- 1/2 sweet potatoes, grated
- 1 bunch of spinach
- 1 bunch rainbow chard, chopped
- Parsley, fresh, chopped

Batter
- 1 cup of oat flour (96g)
- 1 cup of rice flour (96g)
- 1 tsp. of cornstarch
- 1 tsp. of baking powder
- 2 tbsps. Of flaxseeds
- 1/2 tsp. of cumin
- 1 tsp. of salt
- 1 tsp. of nutmeg
- 1/2 cup of tofu (76g)
- 7 tbsps. of oat cream
- 1 cup of oat milk (237mL)

Garnishes
- 2 tbsps. hemp seeds

DIRECTIONS

1. Preheat the oven to 400°F (204℃). Heat a skillet on a medium heat and pour in some of the vegetable stock. Add in the garlic and sweet potato, and sauté for around 5 minutes. Add in the spinac, and cook for an additional 2 minutes, until the spinach is withered. Remove from heat and let cool.
2. In a large mixing bowl, blend all the dry fixings. Crush the tofu well and add it to the dry fixings.

3. Add into the bowl the cooked vegetables, chard and parsley, and blend well until all fixings are consolidated.
4. Then spoon mixture into a prepared muffin tin. Sprinkle hemp seeds on every muffin cup. Bake for 25 minutes.

Nutritional Facts:
Calories: 141
Proteins: 4.9g
Carbs: 20.5g
Fats: 4.9g

SUPER SAVORY AVOCADO TOAST

Servings: 2

INGREDIENTS

- 1 medium avocado, mashed
- 1 tbsp. of fresh lemon juice
- 4 oz. mushrooms, chopped (113g)
- 1/2 cup cannellini beans (91g)
- 1 oz. microgreens (28g)
- 1 tbsp. of miso paste
- 1 tbsp. of balsamic vinegar
- 4 slices whole-grain bread, toasted
- 1 tbsp. sesame seeds

DIRECTIONS

1. Combine the avocado and lemon juice, and set aside.
2. Add mushrooms to an oiled skillet that has been heated over medium heat. Once the mushrooms have softened, add in beans and microgreens and remove from heat.
3. Whisk miso paste with 1 tablespoon of water in a small mixing bowl. Pour miso over mushrooms and beans. Mix in balsamic vinegar and set aside.
4. Spread avocado on one side of each bit of toasted bread. Spoon mushroom and bean blend on top. Garnish with some sesame seeds and serve.

Nutritional Facts:

Calories: 450
Proteins: 17g
Carbs: 52.2g
Fats: 21.6g

CAULIFLOWER QUICHE

Servings: 4

INGREDIENTS

- 1 cup of chickpea flour
- 1 tbsp. of flax meal
- 1/2 tsp. of salt
- 1/2 tsp. of Herbs de Provence
- 1/2 tsp. of baking powder
- 1/4 tsp. of baking soda
- 1 cup cauliflower, grated
- 1 cup of water
- 1/2 zucchini, sliced in half-moons
- 1/2 onion, red, sliced
- 1 sprig rosemary, fresh, chopped cleaved

DIRECTIONS

1. Combine the dry ingredients in a bowl and set them aside. Then chop the zucchini and onion and set aside as well. Grate the cauliflower until it is a rice-like consistency and add to the dry blend. Now add water and blend well. Stir in the onion, zucchini, and rosemary last.
2. Press the blend solidly into a skillet. Then bake at 350°F (177°C) for 30 mins until the top is browned. Serve either hot or cold.

Nutritional Facts:

Calories: 110
Proteins: 6.6g
Carbs: 17.6g
Fats: 1.8g

WAFFLES W/ DARK CHERRY SAUCE

Servings: 4

INGREDIENTS

- 1 cup of buckwheat flour (96g)
- 1 cup of wholewheat flour (113g)
- 1 tbsp. of baking powder
- 1 tsp. of baking soda
- 1 pinch of salt
- 1 pinch of cinnamon
- 2 flax eggs [1 tbsp. flaxseed mixed w/ 2 tbsps. warm water]
- 2 tbsps. maple syrup
- 1.5 cups non-dairy milk, your preference (355mL)
- 3 tbsps. apple sauce

Syrup
- 2 cups pitted cherries, dark (300g)
- 3 tbsps. maple syrup

DIRECTIONS

1. Place all of the waffle ingredients in a bowl and mix thoroughly. Heat waffle iron to high.
2. Then pour waffle batter into your waffle iron and cook for two minutes. When done place onto a plate.
3. Mix all the syrup ingredients in a saucepan. Mix well until combined and cook until heated through. Serve drizzled over the waffles.

Nutritional Facts:
Calories: 427
Proteins: 16.2g
Carbs: 76.6g
Fats: 8.5g

VEGETABLE QUINOA BOWL

Servings: 1

INGREDIENTS

- 3.5oz extra firm tofu, crumbled (100g)
- 1/2 cup broccoli, chopped (76g)
- 1/4 cup cherry tomatoes, quartered (38g)
- 1/4 cup mushrooms, sliced (43g)
- 1 cup kale, torn (107g)
- 1/2 cup carrot, grated (42g)
- 1/2 tsp. yellow curry powder
- 1/4 tsp. garlic powder
- 1/4 tsp. onion powder
- 1/4 tsp. paprika
- 1/4 tsp. salt
- 1/8 tsp. pepper
- 1 lime, divided
- 1/2 cup cooked quinoa (89g)
- 1/4 avocado, sliced
- 1/4 cup microgreens (21g)

DIRECTIONS

1. Heat a pan on a medium to high heat. Combine all the seasonings together in a small bowl. When the pan is hot add in the broccoli, carrot, and mushrooms with a little water. Let cook until the vegetables are tender.
2. Lower the heat to medium and add in the kale, cherry tomatoes, and seasoning. Sauté mixture until the kale has wilted.
3. Squeeze in the lime juice. Then add in the tofu and scramble with the vegetables until the tofu is warmed through and begins to brown. When done, spoon over cooked quinoa in your bowl and begin assembling.
4. Top the vegetable blend with cut avocado and sprouts. Then squeeze a little lime over the top. Add some salt and pepper to taste.

Nutritional Facts:
Calories: 350
Proteins: 18g
Carbs: 41.5g
Fats: 15.8g

OVERNIGHT OATS W/ BLUEBERRIES

Servings: 2

INGREDIENTS

- ◆ 3/4 cup plant-based milk, unsweetened
- ◆ 1 cup oats, rolled
- ◆ 1/2 cup soy yogurt
- ◆ 1 tbsp. maple syrup
- ◆ 1 medium banana
- ◆ 1/2 cup blueberries

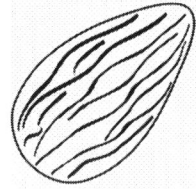

DIRECTIONS

1. Combine plant milk, yogurt, blueberries, and rolled oats in a bowl. Leave them overnight in the refrigerator. In the morning, include one diced banana.
2. Transfer blueberry overnight oats to a bowl and top with bananas, berries, or whatever you like.

Nutritional Facts:
Calories: 280
Proteins: 17.3g
Carbs: 59.9g
Fats: 5.5g

POLENTA W/ FRUIT

Servings: 4

INGREDIENTS

- ◆ 1/4 cup syrup, brown rice (59mL)
- ◆ 2 pears, stripped, cored, and diced
- ◆ 1 cup dried cranberries (152g)
- ◆ 1 tsp. ground cinnamon

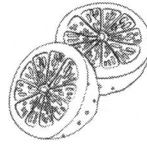

Polenta

- ◆ 1 ½ cups coarse cornmeal (341g)
- ◆ Salt to taste

DIRECTIONS

1. Boil 5 cups of water in a pot. Add the cornmeal to the water, a little at a time while whisking continuously. Cook until the polenta is thick and velvety, around 30 minutes. Season with salt and set to the side.
2. Warm the syrup and add in the pears, cranberries, and cinnamon. Cook until the pears are delicate around 10 minutes. Stir occasionally.
3. Divide the polenta between 4 bowls. Top with the pear compote.

Nutritional Facts:
Calories: 323
Proteins: 5.9g
Carbs: .71.7g
Fats: 3.1g

FUL MEDAMES

Servings: 4

INGREDIENTS

- 1 1/2 lb. fava beans, dried [soaked overnight]
- 1 med. onion, yellow, chopped fine
- 4 cloves garlic, minced
- 1 tsp. ground cumin
- Lemon zest, fresh
- Salt
- 1 lemon, quartered

DIRECTIONS

1. Add the beans to a medium stockpot and cover with water. Bring water to a boil and then lower the heat. Cook until beans are soft (about 1.5 to 2 hours).
2. Sauté the onion in a medium skillet on a medium heat until translucent. Then add garlic, cumin, and lemon zest and cook for a further 5 minutes. Set to the side.
3. When the beans are completely cooked, reserve half a cup of the bean stock and drain the rest. Add the onion blend to the beans. Mix well and season with salt to taste. Serve with lemon quarters.

Nutritional Facts:
Calories: 168
Proteins: 14g
Carbs: 34.5g
Fats: 1.5g

LUNCH ON THE GO

CHICKPEA SALAD SANDWICHES

Servings: 4

INGREDIENTS

- 1 cup red lentils, cooked (61g)
- 1 cup chickpeas, canned, drained (118g)
- 1 celery, finely chopped
- 1 carrot, grated
- 1/4 bell pepper, red and green, finely diced
- 3 green onions, finely diced
- 1 med. pickle, finely chopped
- 3 tbsps. dill, fresh, finely chopped
- 1/2 tbsp. lemon juice, fresh
- 4 tbsps. Mayo, vegetarian
- 3 tbsps. nutritional yeast
- 1/4 tsp. salt, black
- Pepper to taste
- 2 slices of whole-grain bread, sprouted
- 2 leaves of lettuce

DIRECTIONS

1. Prep all the ingredients. Softly squash chickpeas with a fork. Then add in the lentils, finely diced vegetables, mayo, lemon juice, yeast, salt, and pepper. Blend together with a fork.
2. Mix a third of the blend with a blender. Then re-introduce the blend and mix all together with a fork. Then scoop 1/3 cup of the mix on a piece of bread and lay 2 leaves of lettuce on the other cut of bread. Close the sandwich and enjoy!

Nutritional Facts:
Calories: 345
Proteins: 20g
Carbs: 52g
Fats: 7.7g

CURRIED CHICKPEA SOUP

Servings: 5

INGREDIENTS

- 1 tbsp. olive oil
- 1/4 onion, diced
- 3 cloves garlic, minced
- 1 can chickpeas, drained
- 1 tsp. ground coriander
- 1 tbsp. yellow curry powder
- 1 tsp. turmeric
- Pinch of cayenne
- 2 cups vegetable stock(473mL)
- 2/3 cup coconut cream (156mL)
- Fresh lime, squeezed
- water, to thin

DIRECTIONS

1. Heat oil on a medium to high heat in a skillet. Add the onion and garlic, and sauté until softened. Add in chickpeas, coriander, curry powder, turmeric, and cayenne. Cook for an extra 5 minutes. Then add the vegetable stock and cook for 5 minutes.
2. Purée and mix in coconut cream. Mix in lime juice, taste and add more if needed.
3. Serve with a whirl of coconut cream, ground pepper, and pumpkin seeds.

Nutritional Facts:
Calories: 895
Proteins: 1.6g
Carbs: 4.7g
Fats: 101g

GREEK STYLE PINWHEELS

Servings: 16

INGREDIENTS

Tahini Sauce:
- 3 tbsps. Tahini Paste
- 3 tbsps. lemon juice, fresh
- 4 tbsps. vinegar, white
- 1/2 cup water (120 ml)
- 1 clove garlic, minced
- salt pepper to taste

Pinwheels:
- olives
- cherry tomatoes
- artichokes
- lettuce
- tortillas

DIRECTIONS

1. In a bowl, whisk together all the tahini ingredients thoroughly.
2. Cut the tomatoes, artichokes, and olives into desired cuts.
3. Spread around one tablespoon of tahini sauce on one tortilla. Include the vegetables and top with a bunch of mixed greens. Firmly fold the tortillas and cut into pinwheels.

Nutritional Facts:
Calories: 16
Proteins: .6g
Carbs: 3.1g
Fats: .2g

MANGO AND MINT SPRING ROLLS

Servings: 6

INGREDIENTS

- 6 sheets of Vietnamese rice paper
- 1 avocado
- 1 cucumber
- 3 carrots
- 1 mango
- 3 green onions, sliced
- 1 cup cabbage, purple, sliced (152g)
- 6 radishes, cut into matchsticks
- 1 cup crisp mint, fresh (83g)
- 3 cups lettuce, sliced (455g)
- 1 cup glass noodles, cooked (178g)

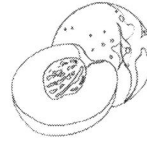

Fried Sesame Tofu:
- 7 oz. firm tofu (199g)
- 1 tsp. sesame oil
- 1 tbsp. soy sauce
- 1 tbsp. sesame seeds

Dipping Sauce:
- 1/4 cup peanut butter, chunky (63g)
- 2 tsps. soy sauce
- 1 clove of garlic, minced
- 3tbsps. warm water
- 1/2 tsp. sriracha

DIRECTIONS

1. Cut the tofu into strips. Heat the sesame oil in a skillet. Place the tofu and soy sauce in the sillet and cook until the tofu is browned and firm. Throw in the sesame seeds and cook for another minute.
2. Prep the avocado, carrots, mango, lettuce, and cabbage. Fill a shallow bowl with water and dunk the rice papers in water. Try not to let them soak for too long.

3. Now begin filling them with the veggies and tofu and wrap them like a burrito.

4. Put all the ingredients for the dipping sauce in a bowl and mix until completely combined.

Nutritional Facts:

Calories: 313
Proteins: 11.5g
Carbs: 41g
Fats: 13.5g

ZOODLE BOWL

Servings: 2

INGREDIENTS

- 2 zucchini, spiralized
- 1/2 cucumber, spiralized
- 1/2 bell peppers, red, chopped
- 1/2 bell pepper, yellow, chopped
- 7 cherry tomatoes, halved
- 3 tbs. onion, red, chopped
- 1/4 cup artichokes, chopped
- Parsley, fresh, chopped
- 1 sprig, mint, chopped
- 3 tbsps. hemp hearts

Dressing

- 1/2 tsp. garlic powder
- 1 tsp. Italian seasoning
- 1/4 tsp. salt
- 1/2 tbsps. vinegar, red wine
- 1/2 tbsps. olive oil
- 1 sprig mint, chopped

DIRECTIONS

1. Spiralize the zucchini and cucumber place in two dishes. Prep the veggies and herbs, dole them out between the two dishes. Then add the hemp hearts.
2. Make the dressing and put in a small container with a tight-fitting lid. Add in the seasoning, red wine vinegar, olive oil, and mint. Shake well. Then pour dressing over a plate of mixed greens.

Nutritional Facts:
Calories: 144
Proteins: 3.2g
Carbs: 27.1g
Fats: 3.9g

PARTY TIME

CAULIFLOWER BITES W/ RANCH

Servings: 6

INGREDIENTS

Batter
- 3 tbsps. hot sauce
- 1 tbsp. olive oil, extra virgin
- 1/2 tsp. dark pepper
- 1 tsp. cayenne powder
- 1 1/2 tsp. garlic powder
- 1 1/2 tsp. onion powder
- 2 tsp. paprika
- 1 tsp. cumin powder
- 3/4 tsp salt
- 3 tbsp. cornstarch
- 1/3 cup flour(41.67 g)
- 1/2 cup coconut milk, canned (113 ml)
- 1/4 cup water (62.5 ml)
- 4 cups cauliflower florets (1160 to 1300 g)

Breading
- 3/4 cup bread crumbs (81 g)
- 2 tbsp flour
- 1/2 tsp. cayenne
- 1/2 tsp. onion powder
- 1/2 tsp. garlic
- 1/2 tsp. paprika
- 1/4 tsp. salt

Ranch
- 1/2 cup cashew, ground (118.29 g)
- 3/4 cup almond milk (200 ml)
- 2 tbsp flour
- 2/3 tsp salt
- 1 tbsps. olive oil, extra virgin
- 1 tbsp. nutritional yeast
- Pepper to taste
- 2 cloves garlic, chopped
- 2 tsps. ranch seasoning
- 2 tsps. vinegar, apple cider
- 1 tsp. celery seeds

DIRECTIONS

1. Preheat the oven to 425 ℉ (220ºC).
2. In a bowl, blend everything for the batter, except for the cauliflower.
3. In another shallow bowl, blend everything under breadcrumb heading. Dunk cauliflower in the batter, then coat thoroughly in the breadcrumbs and place on a baking sheet lined with parchment. Sprinkle any extra batter on the cauliflower. Drizzle with oil.
4. Bake for 25 minutes. Test with a toothpick. If it removes easily from the cauliflower, it's ready. Serve warm with a dip.
5. Mix everything except for the celery seeds. Taste and modify salt and flavor. Include celery seeds and stir until mixed thoroughly. Chill and serve.

Nutritional Facts:
Calories: 334
Proteins: 8.5g
Carbs: 35.4g
Fats: 19.2g

SPICE BROCCOLI FRITTERS

Servings: 2

INGREDIENTS

- 2.5 cups broccoli florets, chopped
- 1/4 cup onion, chopped fine(40 g)
- 1/4 cup cilantro, chopped (4 g)
- 1/3 tsp. salt
- 1/2 tsp. garlic powder
- 1/2 tsp. paprika
- 1 tsp. chipotle powder
- 1 tsp. oil
- 1 tbsp. bar-b-que sauce
- 3/4 cup chickpea flour (90 g)

DIRECTIONS

1. Process the broccoli, onion, and cilantro in a food processor. Move to a bowl. Include the remaining ingredients and blend. Blend well until combined. Let sit for two minutes for the broccoli to dry out. Form 6 patties.
2. Warm a skillet over medium heat. Include a touch of oil and butter. Sauté the patties for 4 to 5 minutes on each side. Serve with sriracha, ketchup, bar-b-que sauce, marinara or ranch.

Nutritional Facts:
Calories: 248
Proteins: 17.1g
Carbs: 31.8g
Fats: 5.9g

BAKED FRIES VIETNAMESE STYLE

Servings: 3

INGREDIENTS

- 1 large sweet potato cut into matchsticks
- 1/3 cup roasted cashews pieces
- Cilantro, fresh, chopped
- Basil, fresh, chopped
- Scallions, fresh, chopped
- Mung bean sprouts
- Sriracha
- Vegan mayo thinned out

Chili sauce

- 1 1/2 tbsp. rice vinegar
- 1 tbsp. white vinegar
- 2 tbsps. soy sauce
- 1/2 tsp. garlic powder
- 1 tsp. ginger, minced
- 1/4 tsp. pepper
- 2 tbsps. sambal oelek
- 3 tbsps. sugar
- 1 tsp. cornstarch
- 3 tbsps. more water

DIRECTIONS

1. Bake the sweet potato. The heat the cashew pieces. Combine all the ingredients for the chili sauce and bring to a boil.
2. Save 1 tbsps. of nuts and then blend the rest in with a large portion of the sauce. Organize the fries on a platter. Sprinkle salt, pepper to taste. Layer cilantro and basil.
3. Include a layer of bean sprouts. Include the sauced cooked nuts. Drizzle the sriracha, vegetarian mayo, and a greater amount of the sweet chili sauce. Then top with scallions, remaining nuts, and more cilantro. Serve warm.

Nutritional Facts:

Calories: 193
Proteins: 4.8g
Carbs: 22.8g
Fats: 10g

BROCCOLI BALLS

Servings: 12

INGREDIENTS

- 1 tsp. oil
- 1/2 cup onion, diced finely(80 g)
- 1 head of broccoli, florets
- 2 tbsp. basil, fresh
- 1/2 tsp. dried oregano
- 1/2 tsp. garlic
- 1/2 tsp. chipotle pepper
- 1/4 tsp. ground pepper
- 1/3 tsp. salt
- 1 tbsp. nutritional yeast
- 1/4 cup almond meal(28 g)
- 1/4 cup bread crumbs(27 g)
- 1 chia seed egg

DIRECTIONS

1. Preheat oven to 400°F (200ºC).
2. In a skillet, warm the oil over a medium heat. Add onions to oil and cook for 3 to 4 minutes.
3. Combine the broccoli and basil in a processor and pulse. Add to the skillet. Toss in some salt and cook until most of the moisture has evaporated. Take off the heat and set aside.
4. Once cooled, you can then add the almond meal and breadcrumbs. Mix thoroughly. Make the flax egg and combine. If still wet, add more bread crumbs.
5. Shape into balls. Place on a prepared baking sheet.
6. Bake for 20 to 25 minutes, until lightly browned. Turn the sheet around 15 minutes into baking. Serve warm with marinara or over spaghetti or as veggie balls in a sub sandwich.

Nutritional Facts:
Calories: 12
Proteins: .6g
Carbs: 1.5g
Fats: .4g

PRETZEL BITES W/ MUSTARD

Servings: 6

INGREDIENTS

Pretzels
- 1 cup of warm water (250 ml)
- 1 tbsp. active dry yeast
- 1tbsp. coconut sugar
- 3 cups unbleached white flour (375 g)
- 3/4 tsp. salt
- 3 tbsp. oil
- 2 tsp. salt

Baking Soda Wash
- 1 tbsp. baking soda
- 1/2 cup boiling water(125 ml)

Cornstarch Vegan Egg Wash
- 1 tbsp. cornstarch
- 1/2 cup water(125 ml)

Spicy Mustard Dip
- 1/2 cup cashews, coarsely chopped(64.5 g)
- 1/4 cup almond milk (62.5 ml)
- 2 tbsps. Dijon mustard
- 2 tsps. hot sauce
- 1 tbsp. nutritional yeast
- salt and pepper to taste

DIRECTIONS

1. Preheat the stove to 450°F (220°C).
2. In a bowl, mix the warm water, yeast, and sugar. Blend and let sit until foamy, about 5 minutes.
3. In a separate bowl, combine the flour and 3/4 tsp salt. Blend well. Add the yeast blend to the flour, include the oil, and work by hand for 4-6 minutes until it forms a smooth mixture.
4. Splash water on the mixture, cover with a towel, and leave it to rise for 60 minutes.

5. Roll out the mixture until it is about a quarter-inch thick. Cut up into strips utilizing a pizza shaper. Cut the strips into 1-inch pieces and form into pretzels. Place the pretzels on the prepared baking sheet about 1/2 inch from one another.

6. Then you will add baking soda to 1/2 cup of boiling water, blend. Brush the pretzels generously with this wash. Let them sit for 2 minutes. Then cut the tops utilizing blade or kitchen scissors.

7. Mix the cornstarch in a 1/2 cup of water. Heat over a medium to high heat until it thickens into a paste. Brush the pretzels with the warm cornstarch wash. Sprinkle granulated salt on the pretzels. Bake until lightly browned, usually 13 -14 minutes.

8. Mix the cashews with the almond milk until smooth. Include more almond milk, if necessary. Add in the Dijon mustard, hot sauce, and nutritional yeast. Mix, taste, and alter seasonings. Serve with warm pretzel bites.

Nutritional Facts:
Calories: 447
Proteins: 11g
Carbs: 60.3g
Fats: 18.8g

BAKED VEGAN MOZZARELLA STICKS

Servings: 4

INGREDIENTS

- 1/2 cup crude cashews, soaked (64.5 g)
- 1/2 cup almond milk(118mL)
- 2 tsps. tapioca starch
- 1 tsp. cornstarch
- 1/4 tsp. agar powder
- 1/2 tsp. salt
- 1/2 tsp. vinegar, apple cider
- 1/2 tsp. lemon juice, fresh
- 1 tsp. nutritional yeast
- 2 tsps. olive oil, extra virgin
- 1 tbsp. olive oil, extra virgin
- A pinch of black salt
- A pinch of onion powder
- 1/4 tsp. crushed red pepper flakes

Breading:
- 1/4 cup flour (31g)

Breading Wet:
- 1/4 cup water (59mL)
- 1/4 cup almond milk (59mL)
- 2 tbsps. flour
- 1 tbsp. flax meal
- 1/4 tsp each of garlic powder, salt, smoked paprika

Breading Dry:
- 1/2 cup bread crumbs (53g)
- 1/4 tsp. each of salt, red pepper flakes, pepper
- 1/2 tsp. Italian seasoning

DIRECTIONS

1. Preheat the oven to 450°F (232°C).
2. Mix all of the mozzarella ingredients into a smooth puree. Fill a skillet and cook at medium warmth, mixing every now and again to abstain from consuming. Cook for 8-10 minutes until the blend is extremely thick and begins to leave the container.
3. Oil a small loaf pan with oil and put the mozzarella in it. Then even it out utilizing a spatula. Put in the fridge and let cool completely.
4. Place flour on one plate. Mix together all the ingredients under breading wet in a bowl. Do the same with everything under breading dry in a bowl.
5. Remove the cheese from the dish and slice into strips. Roll each cut in flour. At that point, plunge it in the wet blend, then into the breadcrumbs to cover well. Place on a lined baking sheet. When done, freeze for 10 minutes.
6. Remove sticks from the freezer and brush the sticks with oil, and bake for 4 minutes. Then move the baking sheet to the top rack and bake until the breading begins to brown. Then take the sticks out and serve with marinara or other sauces.

Nutritional Facts:

Calories: 307
Proteins: 7.4g
Carbs: 24.5g
Fats: 21.2g

BREADED TOFU STRIPS W/ CHILI SAUCE

Servings: 6

INGREDIENTS

Crispy Tofu:
♦ 14 oz firm tofu (396.89 g)
♦ 1/2 cup flour(62.5 g)
♦ 1/2 tbsp. Sriracha
♦ 1 tbsp. soy sauce
♦ 1/2 tsp. garlic
♦ 1/4 tsp. pepper
♦ 1/3 tsp. salt
♦ 1/2 tsp. sugar
♦ 1/2 cup water (125 ml)
♦ 1 cup breadcrumbs (108 g)
♦ 1/4 tsp. salt

Sweet chili sauce
♦ 1/2 tbsp. soy sauce
♦ 1/4 cup rice vinegar(63.75 ml)
♦ 1/4 cup water (62.5 ml)
♦ 3 tbsps. sugar
♦ 1 clove garlic, minced
♦ 1/4 tsp. garlic powder
♦ 1/2 tbsp. sambal oelek
♦ 1/2 tsp. cornstarch

DIRECTIONS

1. Press the tofu in a kitchen towel to expel extra moisture. Cut into strips. Preheat the stove to 400°F (200ºC).
2. Set up the breading station. In one bowl blend the ingredients from flour through the water until combined in a thick batter. In another shallow bowl, place breadcrumbs and blend in 1/4 tsp salt.
3. Coat each strip with batter and then breadcrumbs. Place each strip on a parchment-lined baking sheet. Splash oil on the strips and bake for 30 to 35 minutes.

4. Blend everything under the sweet chili sauce in a container. Warm over a medium heat until simmering. Take off the heat and pour in a serving bowl. Cool marginally and present with the tofu strips.

Nutritional Facts:
Calories: 182
Proteins: 8g
Carbs: 30g
Fats: 2g

DESSERTS

LUXURIOUS CHOCOLATE CAKE

Servings: 14

INGREDIENTS

Cake
- 3 cups unbleached flour (375g)
- 2⁄3 cup unsweetened cocoa powder (60g)
- 2 tsps. baking soda
- 3⁄4 tsp. salt
- 2 cups unsweetened non-dairy milk (475ml)
- 2 tbsps. vinegar, apple cider
- 1 3⁄4 cups sugar (350g)
- 2⁄3 cup softened coconut oil (160ml)
- 2 tsps. vanilla extract

Filling
- 1 cup pumpkin puree (245g)
- 1⁄4 cup unsweetened cocoa powder (20g)
- 1⁄4 cup maple syrup (60ml)
- 3 tbsps. cashew butter

Ganache
- 6 oz. dark chocolate, chopped finely (170g)
- 1⁄2 cup coconut milk (120ml)
- 2 tbsps. maple syrup

DIRECTIONS

1. Preheat the oven to 350°F (175°C). Coat two round springform dish with softened coconut oil. To make the cake, put the flour, cocoa, baking soda, and salt in a large mixing bowl and mix until combined.
2. In a medium bowl, whisk together the non-dairy milk and vinegar until foamy. Add in the sugar, oil, and vanilla. In batches, utilize an electric blender to combine. Empty the batter into prepared dishes.
3. Bake for around 25 minutes. Take out from the oven, however, leave the cakes in pans and let cool totally.
4. To make the filling, process all of the ingredients in a processor.

5. To make the ganache, put the chocolate in a medium heat proof bowl. Add the coconut milk and maple syrup in a pan over medium-low heat. Cook, mixing periodically until simmering. Pour over the chocolate and mix until softened. Allow to cool to room temperature.

6. Remove the layers from their pans. Place one layer on top of the other on a serving platter and delicately shave off the top with a sharp blade. Spread the entirety of the filling over the top. Replace the other cake layer on the filling. Pour the ganache uniformly and let it drip down the sides. Refrigerate for 1 hour before serving.

Nutritional Facts:

Calories: 433
Proteins: 6g
Carbs: 64.8g
Fats: 18.9g

TROPICAL SHAVED ICE

Servings: 4

INGREDIENTS

- 1 cup sugar (201g)
- 1-quart strawberries, diced
- 1 1/2 cup mango juice (355mL)
- 1 mango, diced
- 1/2 cup toasted coconut (42g)

DIRECTIONS

1. In a medium pot, over a medium heat, boil 1 cup water and ¾ cup of sugar. When the blend has boiled, take off the heat and add 2 more cups of water. Empty the blend into a shallow heating dish and move to the cooler for 5 hours, mixing the blend like clockwork to make ice crystals.
2. In a blender, process the strawberries and the remaining ¼ cup sugar until smooth. Strain the blend and move to a container with a pour spout.
3. To serve, separate the ice into four serving glasses. Pour about a fourth of the mango squeeze over every glass. At that point, pour about a fourth of the strawberry blend over each too. Top with mango and coconut.

Nutritional Facts:
Calories: 398
Proteins: 2g
Carbs: 91g
Fats: 6g

VEGAN APPLE CRUMBLE

Servings: 12

INGREDIENTS

Filling
- 6 med. apples
- 1 tsp. ground ginger, fresh
- 2 tbsps. lemon juice, fresh
- 1/2 lemon zest
- 1/2 cup sugar(100g)
- 2 tsps. ground cinnamon
- 1/8 tsp. nutmeg
- 2 tbsps. cornstarch
- 1/4 tsp. genuine salt

Crumble
- 3/4 cup almond flour (72g)
- 3/4 cup brown sugar, packed (146g)
- 1 cup oats, rolled (72g)
- 1/2 cup pecans, chopped (54g)
- 1/4 tsp. salt
- 1 tbsp. vanilla extract
- 8 tbsps. coconut oil

DIRECTIONS

1. Preheat the oven to 350°F (177°C). Core, peel, and cut the apples. Next, peel the ginger and grind it. Combine all the apples and other filling ingredients in a large bowl. Using your hands, mix until everything is coated.
2. In a different bowl, combine all the crumble mix ingredients together. Add the vanilla and mix. Include the coconut oil little by little.
3. Lightly oil a baking dish with coconut oil. Pour the apple filling into the dish, top evenly with the crumble mix.
4. Bake for 45 to 50 minutes. Serve warm.

Nutritional Facts:
Calories: 218
Proteins: 2.2g
Carbs: 30.7g
Fats: 12g

OATMEAL PUMPKIN COOKIES

Servings: 24

INGREDIENTS

- 1/2 cups rolled oats (36g)
- 1/2 cups all-purpose flour (63g)
- 1/2 tsp. baking soda
- 2 tsps. ground cinnamon
- 1 tsp. ground ginger
- 1/2 tsp. nutmeg
- 1/2 tsp. salt
- 1/2 cup coconut oil, liquefied (109g)
- 1/2 cup brown sugar, pressed (97g)
- 1/2 cup granulated sugar(100g)
- 3/4 cup pumpkin puree (188g)
- 1 tbsp. vanilla

Powdered sugar icing
- 3/4 cup confectioners' sugar (91g)
- 1/2 tbsp. almond milk

DIRECTIONS

1. Preheat the oven to 375 °F (191 °C).
2. In a medium bowl, combine the oats, flour, baking soda, cinnamon, ginger, nutmeg, and salt. In a blender, blend the coconut oil, brown sugar, and granulated sugar on medium-high for around 30 seconds until completely combined. Then add pumpkin and vanilla and incorporate it on low for a couple of moments until completely mixed. Progressively add the dry ingredients, blending on low until consolidated into a batter. Place the bowl in the fridge to chill for 30 minutes.
3. Line two baking sheets with some parchment paper. Fetch the batter bowl from the fridge. Make 24 balls and spot them onto the heating sheet. Lightly press down on the balls.
4. Bake for 11 minutes until lightly browned. Take out from the oven and let cool. After a few minutes, move to a wire rack.

5. Then mix together the confectioners' sugar and almond milk until smooth. Place the treats on parchment paper, dunk a fork into the coating and sprinkle in a crisscross pattern. Let the treats sit at room temperature until the coating is dry, around 20 minutes.

Nutritional Facts:
Calories: 135
Proteins: 3g
Carbs: 18g
Fats: 7g

MILLIONAIRE BARS

Servings: 36

INGREDIENTS

Shortbread
- 1/4 cup all-purpose flour
- 1/2 tsp. salt
- 1/4 cup maple syrup (78g)
- 1/2 cup coconut oil (109g)

Walnut Butter
- 2 cups walnuts (218g)
- 1/2 cup maple syrup (156g)
- 1 tbsp. vegetable oil

Chocolate Layer
- 1/4 cup vegan chocolate chips (38g)
- 2 tbsps. coconut oil

DIRECTIONS

1. Preheat stove to 350°F (177°C). Line a square dish with some parchment paper.
2. In a medium bowl, combine the flour and salt. Then add in the room temperature coconut oil and maple syrup and mix it together with a spoon. Press batter into the dish in an even layer that covers. Bake for around 15 minutes until browned lightly on the edges. Permit to cool for around 15 minutes until room temperature.
3. Toast the walnuts over a medium heat in a skillet. Then add in the maple syrup while continuously stirring. Cook for around 2 to 3 minutes until the maple syrup begins to thicken. After that, move the hot caramelized nuts to a processor. Add in the oil. Process for 7 to 10 minutes until the walnuts structure into a thick caramelized walnut spread. At that point, use a spoon to spread the walnut butter onto the cooled shortbread layer. Spread and press it into an even layer.

4. Put the chocolate and coconut oil in a glass mixing bowl. Microwave in 20-second periods, one after another, mixing after each time, until softened. Pour the chocolate over the other two layers and refrigerate until the chocolate layer is solidified around 60 minutes.

5. Remove the bars from the cooler, run a knife along the edges of the bars to loosen. Cut into 1 inch by 2.25-inch square shapes, to make 36 square shapes on the whole. Eat quickly or refrigerate until serving

Nutritional Facts:

Calories: 107
Proteins: 1g
Carbs: 8.5g
Fats: 8.2g

CHEESECAKE

Servings: 10

INGREDIENTS

Almond Crust

- 1 tbsp. flax meal
- 1 1/2 cups almonds (163g)
- 3 tbsps. coconut oil
- 2 tbsps. agave

Cheesecake Filling

- 16 oz. cream cheese, vegan, room temperature (454g)
- 1 1/2 cups powdered sugar, vegan (181g)
- 3/4 cup coconut milk (177mL)
- 1 tsp. ground turmeric
- 1/2 tsp. ground ginger
- 1/2 tsp ground cinnamon
- Pinchof pepper
- Toasted coconut flakes

DIRECTIONS

1. Preheat the stove to 375°F (191 °C). Place a springform pan on a baking sheet. In a medium bowl, put 3 tablespoons water and flax meal. In the food processor, grind the almonds until they're fine. Move to the bowl with the flax meal, blend in the coconut oil, agave, and vegan egg white substitute until combined thoroughly.
2. Press the crust into the base, and most of the way up the sides of the springform pan. Bake until the outside layer is slightly browned, 12 to 14 minutes. Let cool totally.
3. Include the cream cheese, powdered sugar, coconut milk, turmeric, ginger, cinnamon, and pepper to the processor and pulse until smooth.
4. Empty the filling into the crust and move to the cooler. Chill until the filling is set, 2 to 3 hours. Leave the cheesecake chilled until you're prepared to serve. To serve, dust with turmeric, and present with toasted coconut pieces.

Nutritional Facts:

Calories: 172
Proteins: 5g
Carbs: 8g
Fats: 15g

LEMON CAKE

Servings: 10

INGREDIENTS

Crust
- 2 1/2 cups walnuts (272g)
- 1 cup pitted dates (152g)
- 2 tbsps. maple syrup

Filling
- 3 cups riced cauliflower (525g)
- 3 avocados, divided and pitted
- 1 1/2 cups pineapple, crushed (473g)
- 3/4 cup maple syrup (234g)
- Zest and juice of 1 lemon, fresh
- 1/2 tsp. vanilla extract
- 1/2 tsp lemon extract
- Touch of cinnamon

Topping
- 1 1/2 cups plain coconut yogurt (376g)
- 1 tsp. vanilla extract
- 3 tbsps. maple syrup

DIRECTIONS

1. Spot the external ring of a 9-inch springform dish on a lined heating sheet. In the food processor bowl, pulse the walnuts until fine. Include the dates and maple syrup, and pulse until the blend meets up, around 1 moment.
2. Move the blend to the readied springform ring. Press it into an even layer. In the food processor, join the cauliflower rice with the avocados, pineapple, maple syrup, lemon zest, and lemon juice. Pulse until the blend is smooth.
3. Include the vanilla concentrate, lemon concentrate, and cinnamon; beat to consolidate. Empty the blend into the readied dish over the covering. Move to the cooler and freeze until exceptionally firm (around 5 hours and up to medium-term).

4. Take the cake from the cooler and leave to rest at room temperature for 15 to 20 minutes. Remove the external ring from the cake. In a medium bowl, whisk the yogurt, vanilla concentrate and maple syrup together. Pour over the cake and spread into an even layer.

Nutritional Facts:
Calories: 244
Proteins: 3g
Carbs: 23g
Fats: 18g

EASY BROWNIES

Servings: 12

INGREDIENTS

- 2 cups dates, pitted (400g)
- 1/4 cup warm water (60mL)
- 1/2 cup salted peanut butter(128g)
- 2 tbsps. Softened coconut oil
- 1/3 cup unsweetened cocoa powder(32g)
- 1/3 cup vegan chocolate chips (60g)
- 1/2 cup pecans, chopped (60g)

DIRECTIONS

1. Preheat oven to 350℉ (176℃). Line a standard baking dish with parchment paper. Set aside.
2. Add dates to a processor and dice until dates are finely diced. When diced, form the dates into balls. Then add boiling water and mix until a date glue forms.
3. Include peanut butter, coconut oil, and cacao powder and process until it forms a sticky batter. Now include chocolate chips and pecans then process until mixed thoroughly.
4. Move the batter to a lined container and spread into an even layer.
5. Bake for 15 mins on the middle rack. Once done, allow to cool. Carefully take out of the and leave to cool on a plate. The more they cool, the firmer they will get. Cut and serve.

Nutritional Facts:

Calories: 215
Proteins: 3.6g
Carbs: 36.7g
Fats: 8.1g

SALTED BUTTERSCOTCH TART

Servings: 10

INGREDIENTS

Shortbread Crust
- 1/2 cup granulated sugar (100g)
- 1/4 cup virgin coconut oil (55g)
- 1 tsp. vanilla extract
- 2 cups almond flour (192g)
- 1/2 tsp. salt

Filling
- 2/3 cup coconut sugar (150g)
- 2/3 cup canned coconut cream (166g)
- 1/2 cup coconut oil (109g)
- 1 tsp. salt
- Flake salt
- 1 Granny Smith apple, cut

DIRECTIONS

1. Preheat the oven to 375°F (191°C). In a bowl with a handheld blender, blend the granulated sugar, coconut oil, and vanilla together until feathery. Blend in the almond flour and salt. Press the blend equally into around the whole tart dish.
2. Place the dish in the fridge for 10 minutes to solidify, and then bake for 15 minutes. Remove from the stove and let cool.
3. In a pan, combine the brown sugar, coconut cream, coconut oil, and salt. Heat to the point of boiling and afterward cook over medium warmth for around 25 minutes. Have some ice water close by. Plunge the tip of a fork into the bubbling sugar and afterward into the ice water; if the sugar sticks between the tines of the fork without dissolving, the filling is prepared. Empty it into the cooled tart crust, sprinkle with sea salt, place the apple cuts on the top and let it cool. Cut and serve.

Nutritional Facts:
Calories: 431
Proteins: 6g
Carbs: 32g
Fats: 33g

BANANA NUT SCONES

Servings: 8

INGREDIENTS

Scones
♦ 1 cup pecans, chopped (109g)
♦ 2 cups whole wheat flour (226g)
♦ 1 tbsp. baking powder
♦ 1 tsp. cinnamon
♦ 1/2 tsp. ground ginger
♦ 1/2 tsp. salt
♦ 1/3 cup coconut oil (72g)
♦ 3/4 cup banana, crushed (162g)
♦ 1/4 cup almond milk (61g)
♦ 2 tbsps. maple syrup
♦ 1/2 tsp. vanilla extract

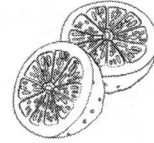

Maple glaze
♦ 1 cup powdered sugar (121g)
♦ 1/8 tsp. salt
♦ 1 tbsp. liquefied coconut oil
♦ 1/2 tsp. vanilla
♦ 1/4 cup maple syrup, include more if necessary (78g)

DIRECTIONS

1. Preheat stove to 425 ℉ (246 ℃). Layer the nuts in a layer on a rimmed parchment-lined baking sheet. Toast the nuts in the stove until fragrant, about 3 minutes. Cleave the nuts into fine pieces.
2. In a medium blending bowl, add the flour, three quarters of the cleaved nuts, baking powder, cinnamon, ginger, and salt and whisk together. Cut the coconut oil into the dry ingredients. In a measuring cup, measure three-quarters of a cup of crushed banana. Include milk until you have a sum of 1 cup fluid. Pour in maple syrup and vanilla extract and blend well.
3. Empty the banana mixture into the dry ingredients. Mix well with a spoon. On a level surface, structure mixture into a layer that is about an inch all around. Utilize a knife to cut the dough into 8 even cuts.
4. Separate and place on a lined baking sheet. Bake for 15 to 17 minutes or until browned lightly.

5. While the scones are baking, whisk together the glaze ingredients in a little bowl until smooth and rich. Let the scones cool for a couple of moments, then drizzle with glaze. While the coating is wet, sprinkle it with chopped nuts.

Nutritional Facts:
Calories: 435
Proteins: 5.2g
Carbs: 65g
Fats: 18g

DINNER

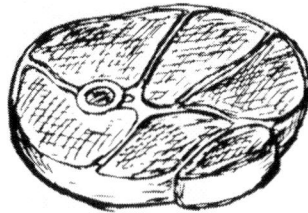

POTATO AND CHICKPEA GREEN CURRY

Servings: 4

INGREDIENTS

Sauce
- 2 tsps. coconut oil
- 1/2 onion, yellow, diced
- 2 cloves garlic, minced
- 1 tbsp. ginger, fresh, minced
- 1 jalapeno, minced
- 3 tbsps. green curry paste
- 2 tbsps. lime juice, fresh
- 2 tsps. sugar
- 1 cup of coconut milk (237mL)
- 1/3 cup cilantro, fresh, chopped (35g)

Curry base
- 1/2 lb. potatoes, diced
- 1 can chickpeas, drained and washed
- 2 tsps. olive oil
- 1/2 onion, yellow, diced

Serving
- 2 cups of cooked brown rice (356g)
- Toasted coconut
- Cilantro, fresh, chopped

DIRECTIONS

1. Heat a heavy-bottomed skillet with coconut oil over medium heat. Add the jalapeño and onion to the skillet, cook until fragrant and tender. Mix in the garlic and ginger, and cook for one more minute. Combine the rest of the sauce ingredients, bringing to a simmer. Transfer sauce into a food processor and blend until smooth. Set to the side and rinse skillet out.
2. Return the pot to the stove. Add olive oil, potatoes, and onions to the pot. Sauté for 8 to 10 minutes. Mix in the chickpeas and the curry sauce. Bring to a simmer and cook until the potatoes are cooked completely.

3. Divide rice between four bowls and spoon the curry on top. Sprinkle with toasted coconut and cilantro before serving.

Nutritional Facts:

Calories: 532
Proteins: 16g
Carbs: 74.5g
Fats: 21.2g

ROASTED TOMATOES AND GARLIC PASTA

Servings: 4

INGREDIENTS

- 3 cups grape tomatoes, halved (450g)
- 10 oz. Vegan whole wheat pasta(283g)
- Olive oil
- 2 medium shallots, diced
- 8 cloves garlic, minced
- salt and pepper to taste
- 3 tbsps.all-purpose flour
- 2 1/2 cups unsweetened almond milk(600mL)
- 3 tbsps. nutritional yeast

DIRECTIONS

1. Preheat stove to 400°F (204°C). In a small bowl, toss tomatoes in a touch of olive oil and salt. Organize the tomatoes, cut side down, on a parchment-lined baking sheet. Bake for 20 minutes. When done, set to the side.
2. Cook pasta per instructions. Heat oil, in a large skillet overa medium to low heat. Add garlic, shallots, salt, and pepper to taste. Cook until translucent and fragrant.
3. Mix in flour and blend with a whisk. Once a paste is formed, gradually pour in the almond milk a little at a time. Bring to a simmer and keep cooking for another 4-5 minutes to thicken. Taste and modify seasonings, adding salt to taste, minced garlic, and a little nutritional yeast for cheese flavor.
4. Serve promptly and garnish with additional pepper or basil.

Nutritional Facts:
Calories: 379
Proteins: 11.5g
Carbs: 64g
Fats: 9g

MEATLESS MEATBALLS W/ TURMERIC SAUCE

Servings: 6

INGREDIENTS

Meatballs
- 8 oz. cauliflower rice (227g)
- 1 cup cooked quinoa, cold (178g)
- 1 cup cilantro, fresh, chopped (107g)
- 1/2 cup flour (48g)
- 4 tbsps. flax egg
- 2 tsp. olive oil, extra virgin
- 1/2 tsp. salt
- 3/4 tsp. allspice
- 1/2 tsp. ground cinnamon
- 3 tbsp. vegetable oil

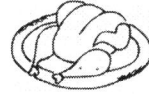

Sauce
- 2 tbsp. olive oil, extra virgin
- 1 med. onion, diced fine
- 4 garlic cloves, chopped
- 1» ginger, fresh, ground
- 1/2 tsp. ground turmeric
- 1/4 tsp. salt
- 1/8 tsp. pepper
- 1/8 tsp. red pepper flakes
- 1 cup coconut milk (237mL)
- 1 cup vegetable stock (237 mL)
- 2 tbsps. lime juice, fresh
- 1/2 cup cilantro, fresh, chopped (53g)

DIRECTIONS

1. Combine all the meatball ingredients, but not the oil in a huge bowl and put in the fridge for 20-30 minutes
2. Heat olive oil in a skillet. Add onions and cook until tender. Add in the garlic and ginger and cook for a further 2 minutes. Now mix in the turmeric, salt, pepper, and red pepper flakes. Cook for 2-3 minutes

3. Pour in the coconut milk, lime juice, and vegetable broth and let it simmer for 5-7 minutes. Then include the cilantro. Take off the heat and set aside.
4. Heat the vegetable oil in a skillet. Using a spoon form around 22 meatballs. Place meatballs in the skillet and cook over a medium heat, 2-3 minutes per side. Once cooked, put the meatballs in the sauce and simmer for 10 minutes. Serve warm over rice or quinoa.

Nutritional Facts:
Calories: 386
Proteins: 8g
Carbs: 28g
Fats: 28g

LENTIL BOLOGNESE W/ RIGATONI

Servings: 6

INGREDIENTS

- 3/4 cup dry green lentils (110g)
- 1/2 tsp. salt
- 1 lb. vegan rigatoni
- 2 tbsp. olive oil, extra virgin
- 2 tbsp. tomato paste
- 1 med. onion, diced
- 4 garlic cloves, chopped
- 1 can crushed tomatoes
- 1/4 tsp. red pepper flakes
- 1 pkg. baby spinach, fresh

DIRECTIONS

1. Put the lentils in a medium-size pan with five cups of water and 1 teaspoon of salt. Heat to the point of boiling, bring down the heat to medium, and keep simmering until the lentils are soft but not mushy.
2. While the lentils are cooking, cook pasta per package instructions. Heat the olive oil in a skillet. Toss in the tomato paste and salt. Cook over a medium to high heat for 3-5 minutes, until the paste begins to caramelize.
3. Toss in onions and garlic, mix and cook for 10-15 minutes until the onion is delicate.
4. Add the tomatoes and red pepper flakes. Heat to the point of boiling, decrease the heat and simmer with the top on for 20 to 25 minutes
5. When the lentils and pasta are cooked, add them to the tomato sauce. Include the spinach and mix well. Keep cooking for 3-5 minutes, until the spinach has shriveled.

Nutritional Facts:
Calories: 469
Proteins: 20g
Carbs: 86g
Fats: 6.6g

BAKED PESTO TOMATOES

Servings: 3

INGREDIENTS

Sauce
- 2 cupsbasil, fresh (213g)
- 1/4 cup olive oil (59mL)
- 1/4 cup cashews, raw (30g)
- 1 clove garlic, chopped
- 1 tbsp. nutritional yeast
- Salt and pepper to taste

Filling
- 1 tbsp. olive oil
- 1 med. onion, diced
- 4 cloves garlic, minced
- 2 tsps. Italian seasoning
- 10 oz. spinach, fresh (283g)
- 3 cups quinoa, cooked (535g)
- Salt and pepper to taste

Tomatoes
- 6lrg. tomatoes
- 1 tbsp. olive oil
- Salt and pepper to taste
- Basil, fresh, torn

DIRECTIONS

1. Preheat the stove to 375 degrees F (190C). Add all of the pesto ingredients to a food processor and blend until smooth and velvety. Set to the side.
2. In a large pan, sauté the diced onion in olive oil until it's tender. Add the Italian seasonings and garlic and cook for a further 2 minutes. Toss in the spinach and cook for 1-2 minutes until the spinach begins to shrivel. Add in the cooked quinoa, pesto cream sauce, salt, and pepper. Mix until combined.

3. Cut the top off of the tomatoes. Utilize a grapefruit spoon to hollow out the tomatoes. Spoon the pesto-quinoa filling into the tomatoes and set the tops back on.

4. Spread some olive oil in a baking dish. Place the tomatoes in the dish and season them with salt and pepper. Bake for 30 minutes, until the skin begins to blister. Serve garnished with new basil.

Nutritional Facts:
Calories: 649
Proteins: 19g
Carbs: 68g
Fats: 37g

VEGAN ENCHILADAS

Servings: 5

INGREDIENTS

Sauce
- 2 tbsps. cooking oil
- 2 tbsps. all-purpose flour
- 2 tbsps. chili powder
- 2 cups water (473mL)
- 3 oz. tomato paste (85g)
- 1/2 tsp. cumin
- 1/2 tsp. garlic powder
- 1/4 tsp. cayenne pepper
- 2 tsp. unsweetened cocoa powder
- 1 tsp. salt

Filling
- 15 oz. can black beans (425g)
- 1 med. avocado, cubed
- 1 tomato, diced
- 2 green onions, sliced
- 1 cup whole kernel corn (171g)
- bunch cilantro
- 1/4 tsp. garlic powder
- 1/2 tsp. salt
- 8-inch tortillas

DIRECTIONS

1. Preheat the stove to 350°F (177°C).
2. In a medium saucepan, add cooking oil, flour, and chili powder. Heat the mixture over a medium heat until simmering. Whisk and cook for 1-2 minutes. Gradually pour in the water while whisking. Then add the tomato paste, cumin, garlic powder, cayenne pepper, cocoa powder, and salt. Stir until smooth. Let the sauce simmer until thickened. Turn off the heat and set the sauce aside.
3. Add the beans to a huge bowl with the avocado, diced tomato, green onion, and a bunch of cilantro. Add them all to the bowl, alongside the corn. Mix everything together. Season with salt and garlic powder.

4. Coat a glass dish with non-stick spray. Fill every tortilla with around 1/3 cup of filling and roll firmly. Set the filled tortillas in the dish, seam side down. When the dish is filled with enchiladas, pour the enchilada sauce over the top.

5. Bake for 25-30 minutes. Top with any cilantro and serve!

Nutritional Facts:

Calories: 303
Proteins: 14.2g
Carbs: 42g
Fats: 6.9g

VEGAN TIKKA MASALA

Servings: 4

INGREDIENTS

- 5 tsps. lemon juice, fresh
- 1 tsp. ginger, ground
- 2 garlic cloves, minced
- 1 jalapeno, chopped
- 3 tbsps. cilantro, chopped
- 1 tsp.chili powder
- Salt to taste
- 1/2 lb. extra-firm tofu
- 2 tbsps. vegetable oil
- 1/2 med. onion, sliced
- 1/4 tsp. turmeric
- 4 tbsps. plain non-dairy yogurt
- 1 cup unsweetened soymilk (237mL)

DIRECTIONS

1. In a bowl, blend the lemon juice, ginger, garlic, jalapeno, half of the cilantro, and chili powder. Season to taste with salt and mix in the tofu until well-covered. Let marinate for 60 minutes.
2. Heat the oil in a skillet on a medium heat and add in the onions. Cook for 3 to 5 minutes, until tender. Gradually include the turmeric, yogurt, milk, and remaining cilantro to the blend. Mix and cook until the sauce thickens.
3. Include the tofu blend into the sauce and cook on medium heat for 5 minutes. Garnish with cilantro and serve promptly with warmed rice.

Nutritional Facts:
Calories: 142
Proteins: 7.5g
Carbs: 6.1g
Fats: 10.7g

Servings: 4

SAUSAGE AND MUSHROOM ETOUFFE

INGREDIENTS

- 1/3 cup unbleached white flour
- 2cups vegetable stock (473mL)
- 1 med. onion, chopped finely
- 1 rib celery, chopped finely
- 1/2 bell pepper, green, chopped finely
- 8 oz. mushrooms, sliced (226g)
- 4 cloves garlic, minced
- 1 tsp. soy sauce
- 1 tsp. dried thyme
- 1/2 tsp. smoked paprika
- 1/2tsp. cayenne pepper
- 1/4 tsp. pepper
- 1/4 tsp. white pepper
- 1/2 tsp. dried basil
- 1 pkg. vegan sausages
- 4 green onions, chopped

DIRECTIONS

1. Add the flour into a skillet and heat over medium-high heat. Cook, mixing continually until it turns light brown, around 15 minutes. Stir constantly to keep from burning. Move it to the blender, include the stock, and mix it until smooth. Set aside.
2. Heat a nonstick skillet on a medium to high heat. Toss in the onion and cook until tender. Then mix in the celery and bell pepper: keep cooking until the onion starts to brown. Now add the mushrooms with a tablespoon of water. Cook until the mushrooms start to release their fluid. Mix in the garlic and cook for one more minute.

3. Give the flour blend another pulse in the blender. Add it to the vegetables. Include the soy sauce and all of the seasonings and cook, frequently stirring, until sauce thickens. Lower the heat and add the sausage. Cook on low for around 15 minutes. Taste to check the seasonings and add more pepper and salt if necessary. Add in the green onions and serve over rice.

Nutritional Facts:
Calories: 301
Proteins: 34.4g
Carbs: 33g
Fats: 5.9g

WHITE BEAN SOUP

Servings: 6

INGREDIENTS

- 2 tbsps. olive oil
- 4 cloves garlic. chopped
- 1 med. onion, diced
- 1/2 lb. carrots, diced (227g)
- 4 stalks celery, diced
- 1lb. dry navy beans (454g)
- 1 entire bay leaf
- 1 tsp. dried rosemary
- 1/2 tsp. dried thyme
- 1/2 tsp. smoked paprika
- Salt and pepper

DIRECTIONS

1. Prep all the vegetables. Add them to a slow cooker with the olive oil. Rinse the beans and then add to cooker. Also add the bay leaf, rosemary, thyme, paprika, and pepper. Cover with water and stir to combine.
2. Cook for 8 hours on low or on high for 4-5 hours covered. Halfway through taste and adjust seasoning.

Nutritional Facts:

Calories: 326
Proteins: 17.8g
Carbs: 53.1g
Fats: 5.8g

CHIMICHURRI TEMPEH

Servings: 4

INGREDIENTS

- 8 oz. tempeh, cut into 8 slices (227g)
- 4 cloves garlic
- 1 cup cilantro, fresh, chopped (107g)
- 1 cup parsley, fresh, chopped (107g)
- 1 tsp. dried oregano
- 1/4 cup red wine vinegar(59mL)
- 2 tbsps. olive oil
- 1/2 tsp. red pepper flakes
- 1/2 tsp. salt
- 3/4 cup vegetable stock(177mL)
- 1 tbsp. soy sauce
- Olive oil spray
- 3 cups rice (535g)

DIRECTIONS

1. Steam tempeh for 10 minutes. Mix everything from garlic to the vegetable stock together until generally smooth. When the tempeh is steamed, pour a large portion of chimichurri sauce and add the soy sauce into a mixing bowl. Reserve the remainder of the chimichurri for pouring over the cooked tempeh.
2. Place tempeh on a plate and pour marinade over it. Rub the marinade into the tempeh. Let sit for 60 minutes, turning halfway through the marinade process.
3. Preheat a large skillet over medium-high. Add a small amount of oil spray. Place the tempeh in and cook until gently sautéed on both sides. Pour in the marinade from the plate and cook for 3 to 5 additional minutes, flipping once. Serve tempeh over rice and drizzle more chimichurri over the top.

Nutritional Facts:
Calories: 202
Proteins: 12.5g
Carbs: 8.8g
Fats: 14g

PANCIT CANTON

Servings: 4

INGREDIENTS

- 1/4 of premade lemongrass marinade (63mL)
- 2/3 cup vegetable stock (167mL)
- 1/3 cup water (83mL)
- 1 tbsp. soy sauce
- 1 pkg. extra-firm tofu, pressed
- 1 tbsp. cornstarch
- 1/4 tsp. salt
- 1/2 tbsp. coconut oil
- 1 cup broccoli florets (65 grams)
- 1 cup snap peas (106 grams)
- 2/3 cup sliced carrot (77 grams)
- 1 clove garlic, minced
- 2 cups Chinese cabbage, chopped (107 grams)
- 115 grams vegan thin noodle pasta
- Roasted peanuts, chopped
- Green onion, cut
- Bean sprouts

DIRECTIONS

1. Prep all the vegetables and sauce. Whisk together lemongrass marinade, vegetable broth, water, and soy sauce. Press extra-firm tofu and then cut into cubes. Put the cubed tofu into a medium-sized bowl, sprinkle with cornstarch and salt. Mix to coat the tofu evenly.

2. In a wok, warm some coconut oil over a medium to high heat. Add the tofu and cook until browned lightly. Turn the heat up to high. Then add extra oil and the broccoli florets and sauté for a minute. Now toss in the carrot and snap peas. Let cook for a minute and then add garlic. Once the garlic is fragrant, add in the cabbage.

3. Include the cooked noodles and sauce. Cover and cook for 2 minutes. Stir and return cover; cooking for another two minutes
4. Serve topped with peanuts, green onion, and bean sprouts.

Nutritional Facts:
Calories: 412
Proteins: 6.8g
Carbs: 5.9g
Fats: 42.5g

ORZO BAKE

Servings: 6

INGREDIENTS

- 1 cup orzo (200g)
- 7 oz. spinach, fresh, chopped (200g)
- 4 spring onions, chopped
- 1 tbsp. oregano, fresh, chopped

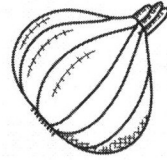

Almond Feta:

- 1/2 cups ground almonds (150g)
- 1/4 cup lemon juice, fresh (60ml)
- 1/2 cup water (125ml)
- 3 tbsps. olive oil, extra virgin
- 2 cloves garlic, minced
- 1/4 tsp. salt

DIRECTIONS

1. Preheat the stove to 350 °F (180 °C). Cook vegan pasta according to the directions. When there are only two or three minutes left, include the spinach and cook until it just shrinks. Drain.
2. Place all the almond feta ingredients in a blender and pulse until very smooth.
3. Return orzo/spinach mix to the pot and pour over the almond feta, the spring onions, and oregano; mix well.
4. Grease dish with vegan butter. Spoon the pasta into the dish, level off the top. Bake for 30 minutes. Remove from oven, cut and serve.

Nutritional Facts:

Calories: 341
Proteins: 10.5g
Carbs: 33g
Fats: 19.7g

LENTIL STUFFED EGGPLANT

Servings: 4

INGREDIENTS

Eggplants
- 4 sm. eggplants
- 2 tbsps. coconut oil
- 1 pinch salt

Lentils
- 1 pkg. green lentils
- 3 cloves garlic. Chopped
- 1 bell pepper, red. Diced
- 2 tbsps. maple syrup
- 1/2 tsp salt
- 1 tbsp. smoked paprika
- 1 tsp. ground cumin
- 1/2 tsp. ground coriander
- 1 tsp. ground ginger
- 1/2 tsp ground turmeric
- 1/2 tsp. cayennepepper
- 1 1/2tbsps. lemon juice, fresh
- 1 3/4 cups crushed tomatoes (375g)
- Salt and pepper to taste
- 1/2 tsp. smoked paprika

Topping
- 1/2 tbsp. vegetarian parmesan cheddar
- 1/2 tbsp. bread crumbs

Serving
- Cilantro, fresh, chopped

DIRECTIONS

1. Preheat stove to 375 ℉ (190 ℃).
2. Cook lentils. Add everything from garlic to the lemon juice to a blender and pulse. Once lentils are cooked, add mixture and mix thoroughly. Set lentils to the side.
3. To a large skillet, add lentils, tomatoes, salt, pepper, and paprika. Heat over medium until simmering. Lower the heat and cook for 5 minutes more. Adjust seasonings.

4. Utilize a blade to remove the meat of your eggplants. Leave enough eggplant substance, so it's durable enough to hold the lentils. Warm a large skillet over a medium heat. When hot, include oil and the eggplant meat side down. Cook on one side for 4-5 minutes until marginally singed. At that point, flip the eggplant over on the opposite side and cook for 4-5 minutes more.

5. When the eggplant is cooked, place cut-side up in a baking dish. Top the eggplants with lentils. Top with veggie lover parmesan and bread crumbs. Bake for 30-35 minutes, until the eggplant is delicate and caramelized.

6. Top with cilantro and serve.

Nutritional Facts:

Calories: 429
Proteins: 19.4g
Carbs: 72.8g
Fats: 9.6g

VEGGIE BURGERS

Servings: 5

INGREDIENTS

- 1 cup brown rice, cooked (155g)
- 1 cup pecans, raw, processed
- 1/2 tbsp. avocado oil
- 1/2 med. onion, diced fine
- 1 tbsp. each of chili powder, cumin powder, and smoked paprika
- Salt and pepper to taste
- 1 tbsp. coconut sugar
- 1/2 cup black beans, cooked (227g)
- 1/3 cup bread crumbs (22g)
- 4 tbsps. veggie lover BBQ sauce

DIRECTIONS

1. Cook rice per instructions. Warm skillet over medium heat. When hot, add in pecans and toast until fragrant and brown. Let cool. Meanwhile, heat another skillet over medium heat. When hot, throw in the oil and onion. Season with a touch of salt and pepper and sauté until onion is fragrant. Remove from heat; set aside.
2. When pecans are cooled, add to processor with chili powder, cumin, smoked paprika, salt, pepper, and coconut sugar and mix until a fine grain. Set aside.
3. In a large bowl, add the beans and pound well with a fork. Next include cooked rice, zest, pecan blend, onion, bread crumbs, BBQ sauce, and until mixture comes together. Taste and modify seasonings if needed. Then form patties, placing them on a lined baking sheet.
4. Heat a skillet over medium heat. When skillet is hot, add simply enough oil to coat the skillet. Place patties in skillet. Cook for 3-4 minutes on each side. Remove burgers from heat, Serve garnished with your favorite burger toppings.

Nutritional Facts:

Calories: 314
Proteins: 9.4g
Carbs: 36.5g
Fats: 15.9g

GRILLED JERK EGGPLANT

Servings: 8

INGREDIENTS

Eggplant
- 1 tsp. ground cinnamon
- 1 tbsp. ground coriander
- 1/4 tsp lime zest, fresh
- 1/4 tsp.cayenne pepper
- Salt and pepper to taste
- 2tbsps. thyme, fresh, chopped
- 4 cloves garlic, minced
- 1 tbsp. ground ginger, fresh
- 3 tbsps. lime juice, fresh
- 1/4 cup soy sauce (60mL)
- 3 tbsps. maple syrup
- 2 tbsps. coconut oil
- 3 scallions, chopped fine
- 1 med. serrano pepper, chopped
- 1 lrg. eggplant

Sauce
- 1/4 cup veggie-lover BBQ sauce (60mL)
- 1 tbsp. lime juice, fresh
- 1 tbsp. olive oil
- 1 tbsp. maple syrup
- 1 tsp. ground ginger, fresh
- Salt and pepper to taste
- 1 scallion, chopped fine
- 1 pinch of cayenne

DIRECTIONS

1. In a little bowl, combine cinnamon, coriander, zest, cayenne, salt, pepper, thyme, garlic, ginger, lime juice, tamari, coconut sugar, coconut oil, scallions, and serrano pepper. Taste and modify if needed.
2. Cut eggplant lengthwise into steaks (1/2") and liberally brush the two sides with the marinade.
3. Heat up a barbecue to medium-high heat and oil the grill. When hot, toss on the eggplant and cook until browned and marked on both sides

4. Now add the BBQ sauce, lime juice, oil, maple syrup, ginger, salt, pepper, onion, and cayenne pepper to a bowl and whisk to combine.
5. Serve barbecued eggplant over cauliflower rice, with sauce, and garnish with fresh herbs

Nutritional Facts:
Calories: 73
Proteins: 1.9g
Carbs: 9.4g
Fats: 3.9g

SNACKS

BLACK BEAN ROLLED TACOS

Servings: 6

INGREDIENTS

- 1 lrg. onion, diced fine
- 4 cloves garlic, minced
- 2 tsps.cumin seeds, toasted and ground
- 2 chiles in adobo sauce, minced
- 2 oranges, zested and juiced
- 2 cans black beans, drained and rinsed
- Salt
- 18 corn tortillas
- 1 1/2 cups sour cream (355mL)
- 1 jar salsa

DIRECTIONS

1. In a pan over a medium heat, sauté the onions until translucent. Add in the garlic and cook for one more minute. Then toss in the cumin, chiles, zest, juice, and beans. Season with salt and blend in a processor until smooth and thick.
2. Heat tortillas in a small skillet until soft. Spread 3 tablespoons of the bean blend over a portion of every tortilla, then roll and face on a baking sheet seam down. Repeat for all tortillas. Heat a nonstick skillet over a medium to low heat andcook each rolled taco for 3 to 4 minutes. Serve with sour cream and salsa.

Nutritional Facts:
Calories: 84
Proteins: 2.3g
Carbs: 5.1g
Fats: 6.3g

PEA GUACAMOLE

Servings: 4

INGREDIENTS

- 2 cups frozen peas, thawed (341g)
- 1 tsp. garlic, minced
- 1/4 cup lime juice, fresh (59mL)
- 1/2 tsp. ground cumin
- 1 tomato, diced
- 4 green onions, chopped
- 1/2 cup cilantro, fresh(53g)
- 1/8 tsp. hot sauce
- Salt to taste

DIRECTIONS

1. Mix the peas, garlic, lime juice, and cumin in a processor until smooth. Move the blend into a bowl and add in the tomato, green onion, cilantro, and hot sauce. Add salt to taste.
2. Cover and refrigerate for at any rate 30 minutes. Serve

Nutritional Facts:
Calories: 83
Proteins: 4.7g
Carbs: 16.1g
Fats: 1g

TERIYAKI CRUNCH ROLL

Servings: 4

INGREDIENTS

- 1 cup brown rice, short-grain
- 1 1/2 tbsps. rice vinegar
- 1 tbsp. natural sweetener
- 1/4 tsp. salt

Filling

- 1 sm. Japanese yam, cooked
- ½ avocado
- 1 carrot, cut into matchsticks
- 1/2 cucumber, peeled and cut into matchsticks
- 4 toasted nori sheets
- 3/4 cup crispy brown rice cereal (102g)
- 1/2 cup ginger, pickled (73g)

Teriyaki

- 1/2 cup soy sauce (118mL)
- 1/3 cup natural sweetener (111g)
- 2 tsps. rice vinegar
- 2 tsps. ginger, pickled, diced
- 1/4 tsp. garlic powder
- 2 tbsps. pineapple juice
- 1/2 tsp. yuzu juice
- 2 tsps. arrowroot powder

DIRECTIONS

1. Bake yam at 375°F (191℃) until tender. Peel when cool and put aside in a bowl.
2. In a medium pan, include 2 cups of water and rice and cook as per directions. At the point when cooked, move rice into a bowl. With a spoon, mix in the vinegar, sugar, and salt into the rice until sticky. Let cool and set to the side.
3. In a pot over a medium heat combine soy sauce, sugar, vinegar, ginger, garlic powder, pineapple juice, and yuzu. Whisk. Cook for around 3 minutes, then add in arrowroot slurry and whisk. Cook around 30 additional seconds.
4. Place sheet of toasted nori (glossy side down) on the roller. With damp hands, spread out the cooked rice equitably over the nori, leaving ½ inch at the top of the nori uncovered. Sprinkle rice cereal. Flip the sushi over onto plastic wrap lined sushi roller.

5. Place small amounts of cooked yam, avocado, carrots, and cucumber in a line, around 1 inch from the base of the nori.

6. Turn the sushi roller with fillings vertical to your body and gradually lift sides of sushi roller while making little shaking movements to adjust fillings. Completely encase roll and crush delicately. Gradually rock sushi utilizing roller until you have the right shape. Tenderly press to seal. Slide onto a clean surface, and with a moist serrated blade, cut into 1 inch thick cuts. When serving, sprinkle with teriyaki sauce and serve with ginger.

Nutritional Facts:
Calories: 318
Proteins: 6.2g
Carbs: 64g
Fats: 4.5g

CRUNCHY ASPARAGUS SPEARS

Servings: 4

INGREDIENTS

- 1 bundle of asparagus(around 12 lances)
- 2 tablespoons hemp seeds
- 1/4 cup healthful yeast
- 1 teaspoon garlic powder or 3 garlic cloves, minced
- 1/8 teaspoon ground pepper
- Touch of paprika
- 1/4 cup entire wheat breadcrumbs
- Juice of ½ lemon

DIRECTIONS

1. Preheat the oven to 350°F (177°C). Clean asparagus and trim end.
2. Move hemp seeds to a bowl and blend in the yeast, garlic, pepper, paprika, and breadcrumbs. Mix and set aside.
3. Organize the asparagus next to each other in a baking dish and sprinkle with the hemp blend. Bake for 20-25 minutes. Serve and sprinkle with lemon juice.

Nutritional Facts:
Calories: 90
Proteins: 6.4g
Carbs: 11.3g
Fats: 2.6g

STUFFED BABY POTATOES

Servings: 8

INGREDIENTS

Hummus
- 1 can chickpeas, drained and rinsed
- 2 cloves garlic, minced
- 2 tbsps. lemon juice, fresh
- 1 1/2 tbsps. grainy mustard
- Salt and pepper to taste
- 1 cup scallions, chopped (171g)
- 2 tsps. Dijon mustard
- 1 lemon, zested
- 2 tbsps. lemon juice, fresh
- 1/2 tsp. ground turmeric

Potatoes
- 12 sm. red potatoes
- Pinch of smoked paprika
- 1 scallion, chopped fine
- Baby kale leaves

DIRECTIONS

1. In a processor, combine the chickpeas, garlic, juice, mustard, pepper, salt, and 2 tablespoons water. Pulse until smooth.
2. In a bowl, mix the hummus, green onions, Dijon mustard, zest, lemon juice, and turmeric.
3. Steam potatoes. Once done, dip in an ice bath. Cut each potato into equal parts and scrape out the interior, leaving a small divot.
4. Fill each divot with hummus. Sprinkle with smoked paprika and serve.

Nutritional Facts:
Calories: 397
Proteins: 10.1g
Carbs: 90.1g
Fats: 1g

HERBACEOUS HUMMUS

Servings: 8

INGREDIENTS

- 1 cupbasil, fresh (227g)
- 1/2 cup tarragon, fresh (113g)
- 2 cans garbanzo beans, drained and rinsed
- 1 cup vegetable broth (237mL)
- 1/2 cup parsley, fresh (113g)
- 1 lemon, juiced
- 2 tbsps. sesame seeds, toasted
- 2 cloves garlic, minced
- 1/4 cupchives, fresh (57g)

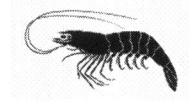

DIRECTIONS

1. Pat the basil and tarragon dry and coarsely chop them. Move to a processor. Add in the beans, broth, parsley, juice, sesame seeds, and garlic. Process until smooth and thick. Serve or refrigerate.

Nutritional Facts:

Calories: 269
Proteins: 1.5g
Carbs: 4,5g
Fats: 28.9g

ONION & PEPPER QUESADILLA

Servings: 4

INGREDIENTS

- 3/4 cup cashews, soaked 2 hours (89g)
- 1/2 cup nutritional yeast (100g)
- 1 lime, squeezed
- 1/2 tbsp. stone-ground mustard
- 1/2 cup water (118mL)
- 1 onion, diced
- 1 bell pepper, red, diced
- 1 bell pepper, yellow, diced
- 1 1/2 tbsps. ground cumin
- 1 1/2 tsp. chili powder
- 8 corn tortillas
- 16 oz. spinach, fresh (454g)

DIRECTIONS

1. Add the cashews, yeast, lime, stone-ground mustard, and water to a blender. Mix until it the sauce is rich. Set aside.
2. Heat a skillet over medium heat. Then add the onion and bell peppers. Mix in the cumin and chili powder. Cook for 5 minutes, then mix in a tablespoon of water and keep cooking. Continue with the water until the onions are caramelized
3. Reduce heat and add the sauce into the onion and peppers. Mix well and cover.
4. Place a skillet over medium heat. Let it heat for 5 minutes. At that point, place one of the tortillas into the skillet. Toast for 2 minutes and afterward flip. Then scoop some of the fillings onto the tortilla and spread it out evenly. Layer spinach over the onions and peppers. Place another tortilla on top.
5. Utilize an enormous spatula to flip the whole quesadilla carefully. Toast the second tortilla for 2-3 minutes. Repeat process. Serve cut into triangles.

Nutritional Facts:
Calories: 394
Proteins: 16.1g
Carbs: 28.9g
Fats: 26.6g

BRUSCHETTA W/ KALE

Servings: 4

INGREDIENTS

- 1 bundle kale
- 1 sm. loaf whole-grain bread, cut
- 1/2 cup cannellini beans (113g)
- 1 cup grape tomatoes, divided (227g)
- Balsamic reduction

DIRECTIONS

1. Put kale in a pot of boiling water. Spread and cook until delicate, around 5 minutes. Drain and squeeze excess liquid out. Toast 8 bits of bread and place them on a platter.
2. Spread a tablespoon of mashed cannellini beans on the toasted bread, at that point layer kale and grape tomatoes on top. Drizzle balsamic reduction over the top.

Nutritional Facts:

Calories: 63
Proteins: 2.2g
Carbs: 13.3g
Fats: 1g

BONUS

PLANT-BASED SNACKS ON THE GO

THAI KALE CHIPS

Servings: 10

INGREDIENTS

- 1 bundle Australian green Kale
- 1/4 cup coconut oil, liquefied
- 2 tablespoons tahini
- 1/2 teaspoon ground bean stew
- 1/2 teaspoon salt pieces

DIRECTIONS

1. Preheat oven to 250 °F (120 °C). Line heating plate with parchment paper. Clean kale and tear into pieces.
2. In a bowl, whisk together coconut oil, tahini, chili, and salt. Pour coconut oil blend over the kale leaves and toss with seasoning blend. Then spread out evenly on the prepped plate
3. Place the heating plate into the stove and bake for 30 minutes.

Nutritional Facts:

Calories: 65
Proteins: 1g
Carbs: 1g
Fats: 7.1g

PAKORAS

Servings: 4

INGREDIENTS

- 2 cups chickpea flour (454g)
- 2 tsps. ground cumin
- 1 tsp. ground coriander
- 1 tsp. garam masala
- 1/2tsp. turmeric
- Touch of chili powder
- Touch of salt
- 1/4 cups water (59mL)
- Avocado oil, for searing
- 1 pkg. kale
- Mango chutney

DIRECTIONS

1. Whisk flour, cumin, coriander, garam masala, turmeric, chili powder, and salt in a bowl. Make a well in the center and add water to it. Mix to combine. Place in the fridge to cool for 30 minutes.
2. Add avocado oil into a wok to coat bottom until it's about a quarter full. Heat to 340°F (170°C).
3. Clean kale and tear into bite-size pieces. Dunk in batter, shaking off the excess. Cook for 3 minutes. Season with salt. Serve with mango chutney.

Nutritional Facts:
Calories: 183
Proteins: 10.1g
Carbs: 27.3g
Fats: 3.3g

PIZZA BLISS BALL

Servings: 2

INGREDIENTS

- ◆ 1/2 cup almonds (113g)
- ◆ 1/2 cup cannellini beans, drained and rinsed (113g)
- ◆ 2 tbsp. oats, ground into flour
- ◆ 1 tbsp. tomato paste
- ◆ 1 tbsp. nutritional yeast
- ◆ 1/2 tsp. Italian seasoning
- ◆ Pinch of Salt

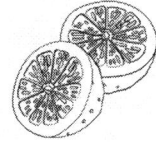

DIRECTIONS

1. Consolidate all ingredients into a food processor and pulse until thoroughly combined.
2. Wet your fingers somewhat and create small balls. Place in a small airtight container and store in the fridge.

Nutritional Facts:

Calories: 104
Proteins: 8g
Carbs: 19g
Fats: 1g

VEGGIE CHIPS

Servings: 4

INGREDIENTS

- ◆ 1 sweet potato
- ◆ 2 red beets
- ◆ 1 rutabaga
- ◆ Sea salt
- ◆ Avocado oil

DIRECTIONS

1. Preheat stove to 300°F (149°C). Line two baking sheets with some parchment paper and set aside.
2. Thoroughly scour vegetables. Utilizing a mandolin, cut the vegetables into chips. Salt and let sit for 15 minutes.
3. Place on baking sheets and bake for 15 minutes. Rotate and bake for another 15 minutes. Remove and leave to cool before enjoying it.

Nutritional Facts:
Calories: 36
Proteins: 1g
Carbs: 8.3g
Fats: .2g

HUMMUS BALLS

Servings: 12

INGREDIENTS

- 2 cups oats (454g)
- 1 cup store-bought hummus (227g)
- 1 tbsp. olive oil
- 1/4 cup chickpeas (57g)
- 1/4 cup sunflower seeds (57g)
- 1/4 cup pumpkin seeds (57g)
- 1/4 tsp. salt
- 1/4 tsp. pepper
- 1/4 tsp. red pepper flakes
- 1 tbsp. nutritional yeast

DIRECTIONS

1. In a huge bowl, mix together everything until combined well.
2. Fold into 12 balls. Store in an sealed container in the fridge.

Nutritional Facts:

Calories: 227
Proteins: 8g
Carbs: 21g
Fats: 13g

CHIA SEED CRACKERS

Servings: 4

INGREDIENTS

- 1/2 cup chia seeds (113g)
- 1 cup water (237mL)
- 1/2 cup pumpkin seeds (113g)
- 1/2 cup slashed walnuts (113g)
- 1/4 cup ground flax (57g)
- 1/4 cup nutritional yeast (57g)
- 1/2 tsp. cayenne pepper
- salt and pepper

DIRECTIONS

1. Preheat oven to 325ºF (163℃) and line a baking sheet with some parchment paper. Combine chia seeds and water and put aside to thicken.
2. In a different bowl, combine the rest of the ingredients. Mix in chia water blend and blend until a batter using your hands.
3. Press batter into baking sheet until ¼" thick. Bake for 30 minutes. Remove and carefully flip the cracker layer. Return to oven and bake for a further 30 minutes or until caramelized and crisp. Remove and let cool before eating.

Nutritional Facts:
Calories: 209
Proteins: 10g
Carbs: 9g
Fats: 16.4g

WHITE BEAN MUFFINS

Servings: 12

INGREDIENTS

- 1 can northern beans, drained and rinsed
- 2 flax eggs
- 1/3 cup maple syrup
- 3/4 cup rolled oats
- 1/2 cup peanut bread
- 1 tsp. baking soda
- 1 tsp. cinnamon
- 1 tsp. vanilla
- 1/2 tsp. salt

DIRECTIONS

1. Preheat oven to 375 °F (191 °C).
2. Combine beans, flax eggs, and maple syrup in the processor and mix until smooth.
3. Add in oats, peanut butter, baking soda, cinnamon, vanilla, and salt and mix once more.
4. Fill muffin tins with batter. Bake for 18-20 minutes.

Nutritional Facts:
Calories: 91
Proteins: 3.3g
Carbs: 12.7g
Fats: 4g

CHEESY CHICKPEAS

Servings: 4

INGREDIENTS

- 1 can chickpeas, drained and rinsed
- 2 tbsps. grapeseed oil
- 2 tbsps. nutritional yeast
- 1 teaspoon crushed rosemary
- 1 teaspoon dry thyme
- 1 teaspoon oregano
- 1/2 teaspoon onion powder
- 1/2 teaspoon garlic powder
- Salt and pepper

DIRECTIONS

1. Preheat stove to 400°F (204°C) and prep a baking dish.
2. Dry chickpeas by moving them in the middle of paper towel sheets and then move to a large bowl. Mix in grapeseed oil, yeast, rosemary, thyme, oregano, onion powder, garlic powder, salt, and pepper.
3. Spread on a baking dish and place in oven. Bake 20 minutes. Remove and let cool.

Nutritional Facts:

Calories: 173
Proteins: 7g
Carbs: 18.4g
Fats: 8.5g

VEGGIE SKINS

Servings: 2

INGREDIENTS

- 2 cups clean and dry vegetable skins (454g)
- 1 tsp cornstarch
- 1 tsp Everything Bagel Seasoning
- 1 tsp olive oil

DIRECTIONS

1. Preheat oven to 400°F (204°C). Place the vegetable skins in a bag and include corn starch. Toss until coated.
2. Add in the Everything Bagel flavoring and olive oil to the pack and toss again.
3. Dump contents onto a lined baking sheet in a single layer. Bake 15-20 minutes. Remove and allow to cool and then enjoy

Nutritional Facts:

Calories: 163
Proteins: 6g
Carbs: 28.3g
Fats: 3.3g

ISLAND TRAIL MIX

Servings: 14

INGREDIENTS

- 2 cups cashews (454g)
- 1/2 cup unsweetened coconut chips (113g)
- 5 oz. dried mango (142g)

DIRECTIONS

1. Preheat oven to 325 °F (162 °C) and spread nuts over a baking sheet. Bake for 10-15 minutes, or until browned and fragrant. After a few minutes, add the coconut.
2. Remove from the oven and let cool. Then add mango.

Nutritional Facts:
Calories: 154
Proteins: 3.7g
Carbs: 14.2g
Fats: 10.1g

DISCLAIMER

The opinions and ideas of the author contained in this publication are designed to educate the reader in an informative and helpful manner. While we accept that the instructions will not suit every reader, it is only to be expected that the recipes might not gel with everyone. Use the book responsibly and at your own risk. This work with all its contents, does not guarantee correctness, completion, quality or correctness of the provided information. Always check with your medical practitioner should you be unsure whether to follow a low carb eating plan. Misinformation or misprints cannot be completely eliminated. Human error is real!

Design: Oliviaprodesign

Printed in Great Britain
by Amazon